The Royal Family

PRINCE CHARLES

IZZI HOWELL

WAYLAND
www.waylandbooks.co.uk

First published in Great Britain in 2018 by Wayland
Copyright © Hodder and Stoughton Limited, 2018
All rights reserved.

ISBN 978 1 5263 0645 6

10 9 8 7 6 5 4 3 2 1

Wayland
An imprint of
Hachette Children's Group
Part of Hodder & Stoughton
Carmelite House
50 Victoria Embankment
London EC4Y 0DZ
An Hachette UK Company
www.hachette.co.uk
www.hachettechildrens.co.uk

A catalogue for this title is available from the British Library.
Printed in China.

Produced for Wayland by
White-Thomson Publishing Ltd
www.wtpub.co.uk

Editor: Izzi Howell
Designer: Clare Nicholas
In-house editor: Sarah Silver

Picture acknowledgements:
Alamy: sandy young 18; Getty: Chris Jackson cover, Hugo Bernand/ROTA/Anwar Hussein Collection 7, Keystone 8, Popperfoto 9t and 12, CaptureLight 9b, Keystone-France\Gamma-Rapho 11, Fox Photos/Hulton Archive 14, Tim Graham 15t and 25, serengeti130 16, POOL/ Tim Graham Picture Library 21t, JoeDunckley 21b, Tim Graham 22, Pool/Anwar Hussein Collection/WireImage 23t, Pool Photograph/Corbis 24, Arthur Edwards - WPA Pool 26; Shutterstock: Frederic Legrand – COMEO 4, 27 and 31, JASPERIMAGE 5b, Lorna Roberts 6, Lenscap Photography 15b, ChameleonsEye 17 and 30, Filipe Frazao 19, Stephen Rees 20, anastas_styles 23b; Wikimedia: Sodacan 5t, Nibaba 10, New Zealand Defence Force from Wellington, New Zealand 13.
All graphic elements courtesy of Shutterstock.

Every attempt has been made to clear copyright. Should there be any inadvertent omission, please apply to the publisher for rectification.

The website addresses (URLs) included in this book were valid at the time of going to press.
However, it is possible that contents or addresses may have changed since the publication of this book.
No responsibility for any such changes accepted by either the author or the publisher.

CONTENTS

Who is Prince Charles?

Charles Philip Arthur George, also known as Prince Charles, is the eldest child of Queen Elizabeth II and Prince Philip. He is first in line to the British throne. One day, he will become king of the United Kingdom.

Prince Charles in 2015 >

Heir to the throne

Charles is the heir apparent. This means that he will become the next ruler of the UK when the Queen dies or if she abdicates. Charles has been the heir apparent since 1952, when he was three years old. This is the longest time that anyone has been heir apparent in British history.

Titles

Charles is often known by his title, the Prince of Wales. This is a special title only given to the heir apparent. He has many other titles as well, such as the Earl of Chester, Duke of Cornwall and Duke of Rothesay. These are also titles that are given to the heir apparent.

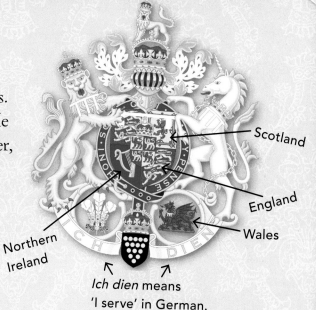

Charles' coat of arms is similar to the royal coat of arms of the UK, with symbols to represent the different parts of the UK. >

Scotland

England

Wales

Northern Ireland

Ich dien means 'I serve' in German.

^
Charles meets people taking part in the Ballatar Highland Games in Scotland.

Royal duties

Charles represents the royal family in the UK and around the world. He meets people and attends the openings of important buildings, such as hospitals and universities. He visits other countries in the Commonwealth and elsewhere to build relationships between the British royal family and foreign leaders. Charles also invites politicians, diplomats and members of other royal families to lunches and dinners when they are in the UK.

DID YOU KNOW?

* Charles has visited over 100 different countries on royal duty, including Afghanistan, Brazil, Jamaica and Australia.

* Charles wrote and illustrated a children's book, The Old Man of Lochnagar.

* Charles enjoys painting landscapes with watercolour paints.

Charles' royal family

Charles has two sons, William and Harry. Together with Charles' wife Camilla and his three grandchildren, they make up part of the British royal family.

Royal parents

Charles' mother, Queen Elizabeth II, has the most important role in the royal family. She is Head of State and Head of the Church of England. She has many royal duties, including opening Parliament and making public appearances at events such as Trooping the Colour (see page 16). In the past, her husband, Prince Philip, joined her at many of these events. Philip is now retired from public duty.

∨ **Charles and his family watch the Trooping the Colour celebrations in 2015.**

Camilla
↓

Charles
↓

George
↓

William
↓

Kate
↓

Queen Elizabeth
↓

Harry
↓

Philip
↓

↑
James, son of Prince Edward

ROYAL DIVORCE

In 1996, Charles and his first wife, Diana, got divorced (see pages 14–15). Divorce has only recently become acceptable for a member of the royal family. In 1936, Queen Elizabeth's uncle Edward VIII had to abdicate because he wanted to marry a divorced woman. He couldn't marry her and still be king. When Edward gave up the throne, Queen Elizabeth's father, George VI, became king instead. However, today, Charles' divorce will not stop him from ruling as king.

Children and grandchildren

Charles had two sons with Diana – Prince William and Prince Henry (Harry). William married Kate Middleton in 2011. After their wedding, the Queen gave them the titles of the Duke and Duchess of Cambridge. William and Kate have three children, making Charles a grandfather. Charles loves reading stories to his grandchildren and does funny voices for all of the characters!

Charles and Camilla smile for a photo on their wedding day in 2005. ⌄

ROYAL TALK

'Grandparenthood is a unique moment in anyone's life ... so I am enormously proud and happy to be a grandfather for the first time.'

Charles spoke about the birth of his first grandchild, George, in 2013.

7

A prince is born

On 14 November 1948, a prince was born at Buckingham Palace. A message posted on the railings of the palace announced the birth of Charles to the world.

Early life

Charles was the first child of Prince Philip and Princess Elizabeth, who was not yet queen. When Charles was born, Elizabeth's father, King George VI, ruled over the UK. Elizabeth had to spend time away from the palace on royal visits overseas and with Prince Philip, who was working for the navy in Malta. Charles, and his younger sister Anne (born in 1950) were looked after by nannies and their maternal grandmother, also called Elizabeth.

In 1953, Charles attended his mother's coronation at the age of four, along with his younger sister Anne. Elizabeth had become queen the previous year, after the death of her father, King George VI. >

ROYAL TALK

'She was quite simply the most magical grandmother you could possibly have, and I was utterly devoted to her.'

Charles talked about his grandmother in 2002.

Off to school

Charles was taught by a governess at the palace until he was eight years old. Then, Elizabeth and Philip decided he should go to school. Charles went to private school in London for ten months. Then, his parents sent him to a boarding school called Cheam, in Hampshire, in 1957. Charles lived, studied and spent most of his free time at school away from his family. However, he could spend holidays with his family at the queen's houses in Scotland and Norfolk.

Eight-year-old Charles (centre) and his classmates walk through the streets of London on a school trip. >

PAST AND PRESENT

Charles was the first ever heir apparent to go to school. In the past, royal children, including Queen Elizabeth II, were taught by private tutors at home. Today, most royal children go to school.

Full board

At boarding school, Charles had to follow a strict routine. He had to wake up at 7.15 a.m., say prayers at 7.45 a.m. and eat breakfast at 8 a.m., before lessons started at 9. When he wasn't in class, Charles played sports, such as cricket. He also enjoyed acting in plays. While Charles was at Cheam, the queen announced that Charles was going to be given the title Prince of Wales.

Prince Charles spent some of his holidays at Sandringham House in Norfolk. >

Growing up

Like many members of the royal family, Charles spent his teenage years at boarding school. His royal duties would wait until he had finished his education.

A new school

At the age of 13, Charles started at a new school, Gordonstoun, in the north east of Scotland. Charles' father, Prince Philip, had gone to the same school when he was a child. The teachers at Gordonstoun were very strict. They thought that they could make their students tough by doing hard things, such as taking cold showers every morning. Charles was not happy there.

Prince Philip has a pilot's licence. He flew the plane that took Charles up to Scotland before his first day at Gordonstoun.

ROYAL TALK

'I hate coming back here and leaving everyone at home ...'

Charles wrote to his family while at Gordonstoun.

∨ Gordonstoun School

New challenges

In 1966, Charles spent two terms as an exchange student in Australia. He enjoyed his time abroad, going on cross-country expeditions in the heat and spotting snakes, leeches and venomous spiders. When he came back to Gordonstoun, he was made head boy. He had more responsibility and tried to help the other students. Before he left the school, he took A Level exams and received a grade B in History and a C in French.

University life

In 1967, Charles went to the University of Cambridge to study archaeology and anthropology. Later, he changed subject and studied history instead. He graduated in 1970 with a 2:2 degree. This was the first time that an heir apparent had graduated from university. While he was at university, Charles spent a term at the University of Aberystwyth, learning Welsh for his role as the Prince of Wales. In his final year of university, he started going to events and representing the royal family when he wasn't in lessons.

∨ Charles enjoyed taking part in drama productions with other students at the University of Cambridge.

A military man

Like his father, grandfather and many other relatives, Charles had a military career. He spent over five years in active service in the Royal Navy in the 1970s. He also holds many honorary titles from the armed forces.

The Royal Air Force

Charles began serving in the Royal Air Force in March 1971. He already had a pilot's licence, so he flew himself to the training centre by plane. He trained as a jet pilot and was awarded his RAF Wings in August 1971.

∧ Charles had to take many flying lessons while training in the RAF.

At sea

In September 1971, Charles joined the Royal Navy. He trained at the Royal Naval College in Dartmouth, where his father and great uncle had also trained. He served on different ships and learned how to organise and lead a ship full of sailors.

He never fought in a war, but he learned skills that a sailor would need in battle, such as escaping from a submarine. Charles also qualified as a helicopter pilot. For the final ten months of his service in 1976, he was given command of his own ship. He was in charge of HMS *Bronington*, a ship that was used to look for and destroy dangerous mines at sea.

MILITARY ROYALS

There is a long history of the royal family serving in the armed forces. During the Second World War, Queen Elizabeth was the first royal woman to join the army, where she trained as a mechanic. Charles' sons William and Harry both trained in the military. William worked as a search and rescue pilot in the Royal Air Force, while Harry served on the front line in Afghanistan twice.

Support for the armed services

Charles stopped his active service in the military in 1976. However, he currently holds many honorary titles, such as Admiral of the Fleet in the Royal Navy, Field Marshal in the Army and Marshal of the Royal Air Force. When Charles becomes king, he will take over from Queen Elizabeth as the Commander-in-chief of the British armed forces. For now, he supports the military in many ways, such as visiting injured soldiers in hospital and being the patron of charities that support people in the military and their families.

Charles meets soldiers on a trip to an army training centre.

∨

Prince Charles sometimes sends personal letters and a bottle of whisky to injured soldiers as a present.

13

Marriage and children

Charles' personal life has not always been easy. However, his two children, William and Harry, have always brought him happiness and pride.

The wedding of the century

In 1980, Charles started a relationship with Lady Diana Spencer. Diana was from a rich family who had connections to the royal family. In February 1981, Charles and Diana got engaged. They got married five months later in July 1981. Their wedding was a huge event around the world. Some people said it was 'the wedding of the century'.

∨ Charles and Diana leave St Paul's Cathedral, London, after their wedding.

7.62 metres – the length of Diana's wedding dress train.

10,000 – the number of sequins and pearls on Diana's dress.

600,000 – the number of people who watched from the streets of London.

750 million – the number of people who watched on TV around the world.

Becoming a family

Charles' and Diana's first child, William, was born on 21 June 1982. Charles was with Diana at William's birth. It was the first time a royal father had been at the birth of his child. Their second child, Henry (Harry), was born on 15 September 1984. The boys came with Charles and Diana on some royal visits.

Charles with William and Harry in 1985 >

Difficult times

Charles and Diana did not always have a happy relationship. They separated in 1992 and got divorced in 1996. Diana was killed in a car crash in Paris in 1997. She was 36 years old. The royal family and many people around the world were shocked and upset. Over a million people took to the streets of London to watch the funeral procession and service, while over two billion watched around the world on TV.

The Mail
ON SUNDAY 85p

FAREWELL: The coffin of the Princess of Wales leaving Westminster Abbey yesterday
THE DAY WE ALL SAID GOODBYE

< Newspapers showed the story of Diana's funeral. Charles, William and Harry walked behind the coffin on the way to the church for the funeral service.

Moving on

After Diana's death, Charles focused on his sons. He helped them to cope with their loss. After the funeral, he kept them away from the public eye while they grieved. As William and Harry grew older, Charles introduced them to Camilla. The princes attended Charles and Camilla's wedding and have developed an excellent relationship with their stepmother.

ROYAL TALK

'She's a wonderful woman, and she's made our father very, very happy, which is the most important thing. William and I love her to bits.'

Prince Harry spoke in an interview about Camilla in 2005.

William

Charles

Official duties

Charles has a busy schedule, working to represent the royal family in the UK and abroad. He is always in the public eye – attending events, meeting people and presenting awards.

∧ Charles and William ride on horseback in the Trooping the Colour procession.

Royal events

As a member of the royal family, there are certain events that Charles is expected to attend. In June, the royal family celebrates the Queen's official birthday with the Trooping the Colour ceremony. Charles rides on horseback in the military parade, along with troops from the army. Then, he watches planes from the Royal Air Force fly past with the rest of the royal family. He also attends the Remembrance Sunday service at the Cenotaph in London every year. Charles lays a wreath of poppies and observes two minutes of silence to remember those who lost their lives in war.

Investitures

Twice a year, the Queen publishes a list of people who she wants to honour for their outstanding public service. Charles and the Queen present these people with awards at ceremonies called investitures throughout the year. They congratulate each person individually and present him or her with a medal. Charles has presented awards to many people for different reasons, including Ed Sheeran and Adele for their service to music and Ewan McGregor for his service to drama.

Overseas work

Charles and Camilla often travel abroad. They are both fascinated by other cultures, and greatly enjoy learning about local traditions. It is part of the couple's royal duties to meet leaders and diplomats, as well as the general public, to show them that the UK is interested in their culture. On his trips, Charles also visits charity projects that he has set up in the past and gathers information to help him set up new schemes.

Charles meets the public on a visit to New Zealand. ∨

Charities

—— •◦• ——

Charles and Camilla are very involved with charitable work. Charles is the president of the Prince's Charities, a group of charities that raise over £100 million every year. This money is used to help people and projects in need, both in the UK and abroad.

The Prince's Trust

After leaving the Royal Navy, Charles wanted to help the lives of disadvantaged young people in the UK. He set up the Prince's Trust, a scheme that helps young people to get into work, education or training. The charity is still going 40 years later, thanks to Charles' and many others' hard work and motivation to help others.

∨ Charles prepares food with people who attend a Prince's Trust workshop that teaches them cookery skills.

ROYAL TALK

'You can see how it is possible to turn young people's lives around and give them self-confidence, self-worth and self-esteem.'

Charles spoke about the importance of the Prince's Trust.

The Prince's Trust has helped over 825,000 people since it was founded in 1976.

∧

The British Asian Trust helps girls in South Asia to attend school for long enough to get a good education.

Helping other countries

The Prince's Charities also help to transform lives abroad. One of the charities in the group is the British Asian Trust, which invests in education, healthcare and employment in South Asia. This helps to improve people's lives in the long run, rather than just giving money as a short-term solution. So far, it has helped over three million people.

Camilla's work

Camilla supports many charities, focusing on issues such as literacy, poverty, homelessness and animal welfare. She has raised awareness of the disease osteoporosis, which weakens bones. Camilla has a personal connection to this cause, as her mother and grandmother both died from the disease. Camilla organises a fundraising walk every year in Scotland to raise money for sufferers of osteoporosis.

Farms and towns

As a child, Charles loved exploring the countryside. Today, he is passionate about farming and protecting rural areas, and the architecture and planning of towns and cities.

The Duchy of Cornwall

As the Duke of Cornwall, Charles is in charge of a huge area of land in the south west of England, known as the Duchy of Cornwall. There are many livestock and arable farms in the duchy, as well as forests and rivers. Farmers in the duchy rent the land from Charles and pay him money. Charles gives this money to charity or uses it for personal costs.

The Duchy of Cornwall also includes farm land on the Isles of Scilly, off the southwest tip of Cornwall.

∨

Countryside and farming

Charles is very interested in farming. He has his own organic farm on the Highgrove estate where he lives (see page 23). He also encourages farmers in the Duchy of Cornwall to grow crops and raise animals in a way that doesn't harm the natural environment, for example by not using pesticides that kill insects. Charles is passionate about keeping farming traditions going in the countryside. He works with charities to help young people become farmers, so that farming knowledge can be passed on to the next generation.

Charles meets schoolchildren on a farm > **as part of a campaign he launched to teach children about where their food comes from.**

Poundbury

In 1987, the town council of Dorchester in Dorset wanted to build new houses on land that was part of the Duchy of Cornwall estate. Charles worked with the council to design the new community, called Poundbury. They thought about how to make Poundbury a good environment for its residents. They built homes near shops and leisure buildings, so that people could walk instead of drive. There are plenty of businesses so that people can find jobs. Many architects and town planners have visited Poundbury to learn about different ways that new communities can be built.

People have moved into the new houses in Poundbury, Dorset, which were partly designed by Charles.

21

At home

Charles has homes in England, Scotland and Wales. He spends time in different houses during the year.

Clarence House

Charles' official home is Clarence House in London. He doesn't actually live in the house, but uses it to receive guests, such as diplomats and foreign leaders, and to host lunches and dinners. Charles did live at Clarence House as a child, between the ages of one and three. Visitors can sometimes take a look inside the house, as it is open to the public for several months every year.

∨ A guardsman and a police officer patrol the entrance to Clarence House.

At home

Charles' family home is Highgrove House in Gloucestershire. William and Harry lived there for much of their childhoods and Charles and Camilla still live there today. The house is surrounded by large gardens in which rare trees and plants are grown organically. Charles has ensured that the house is more ecologically friendly by recycling all waste and planting a reed bed that treats sewage from the house.

∧ Camilla welcomes staff and children from a Welsh children's cancer charity to Highgrove House at Christmas time.

Other residences

Charles also owns other houses, such as Birkhall House in Scotland. This house is on the Balmoral Estate, which belongs to the royal family. Charles inherited Birkhall from his grandmother, Elizabeth, when she died in 2002. Charles and Camilla go to Birkhall on holiday every summer. They enjoy walking in the countryside and fishing. The couple also own a house in Wales called Llwynywermod. They stay there when visiting Wales, and rent it out as holiday flats when they are away.

< Forests and rivers surround Birkhall House on the Balmoral Estate.

Hobbies and interests

Charles has a wide range of different hobbies and interests. He has found ways to mix these interests with his charity work, so that he can support his passions and help others to enjoy them too.

Performing arts

Ever since he was a child, Charles has enjoyed theatre and music. While at school, he acted in plays and played the cello and the trumpet. Today, he works with charities to help children experience the arts. He also attends many theatre and musical performances, sometimes to raise money for charity and sometimes for fun!

∧ Charles meets the cast of the musical *Wicked* in London.

Charles (label)
Harry (label)
William (label)

∧ Charles, William and Harry take part in a charity polo match in 2005.

Polo

At the age of 15, Charles played his first game of polo. Since then, he has become passionate about the sport and has played matches around the world. He also introduced his sons to polo, and both are keen players today. Charles has taken part in many charity matches, which raised a total of approximately £12 million for people in need. He stopped playing in 2005, but still enjoys watching the sport.

Once Charles got hit in the throat during a polo game and lost his voice for 10 days!

Gardening and plants

Charles is passionate about the natural world. He loves gardening in his organic garden at Highgrove and likes to talk to his plants and encourage them to grow strong. Camilla often helps him in the garden. Charles also enjoys planting and shaping plants to form hedges and has laid many of the hedges in his garden himself.

Becoming king

Queen Elizabeth is the longest reigning British monarch in history. When she dies, the heir apparent, Charles, will become king.

∧

Charles joined his mother, Queen Elizabeth II, at the opening of Parliament in 2017.

Handing over power

The Queen has already started to cut back on her royal duties. At over 90 years of age, she no longer has the same energy to attend lots of meetings or to travel long distances. Charles has started to stand in for her at overseas events, such as meetings of the Commonwealth. One day, Charles will take over all of these duties so it's useful for him to observe the Queen.

WHAT'S IN A NAME?

Some kings and queens change their name when they start their reign. For example, Charles' maternal grandfather was called Albert until he became king. After that, he was known as King George VI. Charles may choose to change his name when he becomes king.

Balancing interests

Charles has spoken much more openly about his interests and political opinions than previous kings and queens. Some of these issues can be controversial, such as climate change and alternative medicine. The royal family shouldn't show any political preferences, so when Charles is king, he may not be able to speak so freely about what he thinks. His role as the king will be more important than his own interests.

A new heir

Prince William is next in line to the throne after his father. When Charles becomes king, William will become the heir apparent and the new Prince of Wales. He will inherit the Duchy of Cornwall and the responsibilities that come with it. And one day, William himself will be king.

< Prince William will become the heir apparent when Charles is king.

A NEW QUEEN?

When Charles becomes king, Camilla will legally be the Queen Consort. This is the title for the wife of a monarch. However, Camilla has decided to take the title of Princess Consort instead.

Kings and Queens of England

The House of Normandy

William I *(William the Conqueror)*	1066–1087
William II *(William Rufus)*	1087–1100
Henry I	1100–1135
Stephen	1135–1154

The House of Plantagenet

Henry II	1154–1189
Richard I *(Richard the Lionheart)*	1189–1199
John	1199–1216
Henry III	1216–1272
Edward I	1272–1307
Edward II	1307–1327
Edward III	1327–1377
Richard II	1377–1399

The House of Lancaster

Henry IV	1399–1413
Henry V	1413–1422
Henry VI	1422–1461

The House of York

Edward IV	1461–1483
Edward V	1483–1483
Richard III	1483–1485

The House of Tudor

Henry VII	1485–1509
Henry VIII	1509–1547
Edward VI	1547–1553
Jane	1553–1553
Mary I	1553–1558
Elizabeth I	1558–1603

The House of Stuart

James I (James VI of Scotland)	1603–1625
Charles I	1625–1649
Commonwealth declared	
Oliver Cromwell Lord Protector	1653–1658
Richard Cromwell Lord Protector	1658–1659
Monarchy restored	
Charles II	1649 *(restored 1660)*–1685
James II *(James VII of Scotland)*	1685–1688
William III and Mary II	1689–1694 (Mary)
	1702 *(William)*
Anne	1702–1714

The House of Hanover

George I	1714–1727
George II	1727–1760
George III	1760–1820
George IV	1820–1830
William IV	1830–1837
Victoria	1837–1901

The House of Saxe-Coburg – becomes House of Windsor in 1917

Edward VII	1901–1910
George V	1910–1936
Edward VIII *(abdicated)*	1936–1936
George VI	1936–1952
Elizabeth II	1952–

The royal family tree

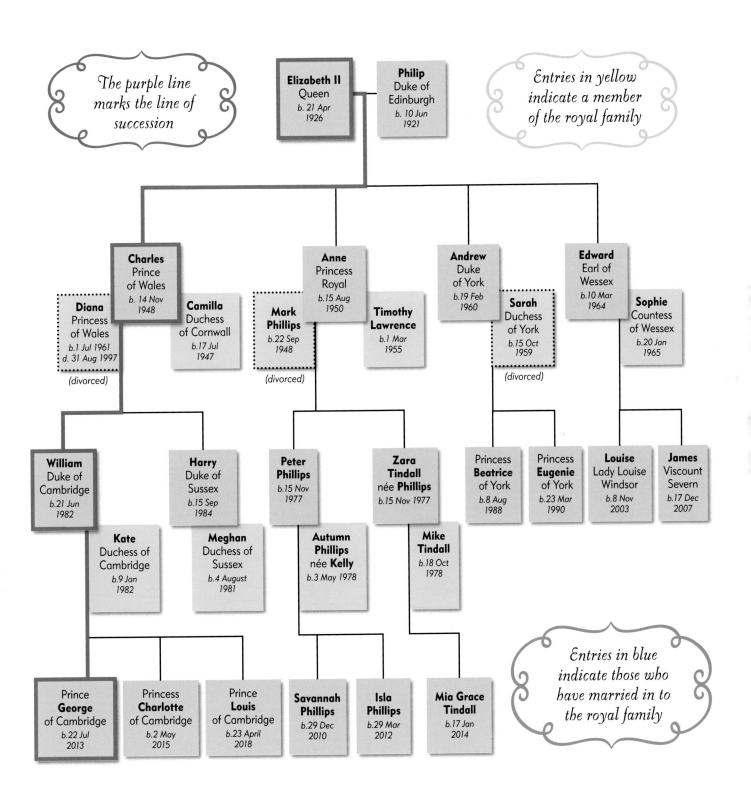

The purple line marks the line of succession

Entries in yellow indicate a member of the royal family

Elizabeth II
Queen
b. 21 Apr 1926

Philip
Duke of Edinburgh
b. 10 Jun 1921

Charles
Prince of Wales
b. 14 Nov 1948

Diana
Princess of Wales
b.1 Jul 1961
d. 31 Aug 1997
(divorced)

Camilla
Duchess of Cornwall
b.17 Jul 1947

Anne
Princess Royal
b.15 Aug 1950

Mark Phillips
b.22 Sep 1948
(divorced)

Timothy Lawrence
b.1 Mar 1955

Andrew
Duke of York
b.19 Feb 1960

Sarah
Duchess of York
b.15 Oct 1959
(divorced)

Edward
Earl of Wessex
b.10 Mar 1964

Sophie
Countess of Wessex
b.20 Jan 1965

William
Duke of Cambridge
b.21 Jun 1982

Harry
Duke of Sussex
b.15 Sep 1984

Peter Phillips
b.15 Nov 1977

Zara Tindall
née **Phillips**
b.15 Nov 1977

Princess Beatrice
of York
b.8 Aug 1988

Princess Eugenie
of York
b.23 Mar 1990

Louise
Lady Louise Windsor
b.8 Nov 2003

James
Viscount Severn
b.17 Dec 2007

Kate
Duchess of Cambridge
b.9 Jan 1982

Meghan
Duchess of Sussex
b.4 August 1981

Autumn Phillips
née **Kelly**
b.3 May 1978

Mike Tindall
b.18 Oct 1978

Prince **George** of Cambridge
b.22 Jul 2013

Princess **Charlotte** of Cambridge
b.2 May 2015

Prince **Louis** of Cambridge
b.23 April 2018

Savannah Phillips
b.29 Dec 2010

Isla Phillips
b.29 Mar 2012

Mia Grace Tindall
b.17 Jan 2014

Entries in blue indicate those who have married in to the royal family

Glossary

abdicate when the heir to the throne steps down and refuses the position

arable a type of farm where crops are grown

coat of arms a symbol that is used by a royal family or a monarch

Commonwealth, the a group of countries, including the UK, that were previously part of the British Empire and share trade agreements

consort the husband or wife of the monarch

coronation the ceremony at which someone is made the king or queen

diplomat someone whose job is to live in another country and keep a good relationship between their government and that country's government

governess a woman employed to teach children in the family's home

graduate to complete a degree at university or other course

heir apparent the first person in line to the throne

maternal a maternal grandparent is one of the parents of your mother

monarch a king or queen

noble describes someone from a high-ranking family, who may have titles and own land

organic describes something that has been grown or raised without chemicals

patron a person who supports an organisation or charity

polo a sport played on horseback in which players hit a ball with long wooden hammers

represent to act on behalf of someone or many people. Prince Charles represents the UK when he attends events and meetings with leaders from other countries

Trooping the Colour a celebration held each year to mark the Queen's birthday

United Kingdom (UK) a country made up of England, Scotland, Wales and Northern Ireland

Further information

Places to see:

Clarence House,
St James's Palace, London SW1 1BA
Charles' official home is open to the
public during August. Visit the garden
planted by Charles and see where he and
Camilla receive guests.
www.royalcollection.org.uk/visit/clarence-house

Highgrove Gardens,
Doughton (Gloucestershire)
The Royal Gardens at Highgrove are
open to the public between April and
October. See the rare plants and trees
chosen by Charles and learn more about
organic gardening.
www.highgrovegardens.com

Websites to visit:

Charles' official website has lots of
information about his life, charities and
interests, as well as details of Camilla's
work: *www.princeofwales.gov.uk*

Visit the website of The Prince's Trust
to find out more about the work that
they do to help young people:
www.princes-trust.org.uk

The official website of the royal family has
details of all its members, as well as royal
residences and events such as Trooping
the Colour: *www.royal.uk/royal-family*

Books to read:

A Royal Childhood: 200 Years of Royal Babies
by Liz Gogerly, Franklin Watts, 2017

The Story of Britain
by Mike Manning and Brita Granström,
Franklin Watts, 2016

Queen Elizabeth II's Britain
by Jacqui Bailey, Franklin Watts, 2015

Who's Who in British History
by Robert Fowke, Wayland, 2014

Index